A Stone's Throw From Chancery Lane

For Gerry + Ruth
With all good wishes
Graham
Matthews
Oct 10

Graham Matthews

Glenthorne Publications

2010
Published by
Glenthorne Publications
Glenthorne, 24 Lower Camden, Chislehurst,
Kent BR7 5HX
email: graham_matthews@ntlworld.com

ISBN 0-9547250-1-8

Printed and bound in the United Kingdom by

Litho Direct

Brighton, E. Sussex, 01273 563111

I dedicate this autobiographical account of my experiences in the spheres of engineering and patents, to my delightful and talented children, Estelle, Ferguson, Candace and Hamilton, in whom I take great pride. This year, the year of family reunion which we commemorate, has been especially exciting for all of them. I wish them good health and much happiness in all they do.

Chislehurst, 1st June 2010

ACKNOWLEDGMENTS

I wish to thank my brother for suggesting amendments to some passages making them less incomprehensible, my wife Daphne for using her as a sounding board and for proof-reading and tidying up the syntax, my neighbour Elizabeth Matthews (no relation) for her expertise and time spent with camera and computer, my former secretary Lorraine Jones for word processing from near-illegible manuscript and my daughter Candace for her professional advice on the production of this book.

An especial thanks to Jill de Warrenne who suggested that I record my experiences as a patent attorney. Her encouragement was invaluable.

A final vote of thanks goes posthumously to my former headmaster, Geoffrey Turberville, who prematurely terminated my formal education at Eltham College in 1949 but who redeemed himself by permitting me to use the school chapel for my marriage in 1957.

PREFACE

Patent attorneys are hybrid creatures. They are a cross between engineers and lawyers qualified to act for inventors before the Patent Office or Patents Court. I set out to record my involvement with inventors and their inventions many of which achieved commercial success and many did not. However, my thoughts soon turned to how I came to my chosen career following the lack of academic success at school. I cannot praise the apprenticeship system highly enough. I am strongly of the view that university, as excellent as it is for many, is not necessarily the sole route to making a useful contribution to society and commerce, in addition, of course, to earning a crust. By means of this book I hope to support this view and at the same time entertain.

Chapter 1

DISMISSED!

It was all on account of a phone call from the Headmaster to my father, that I pursued a career in the world of intellectual property rights. Having spent a splendid year in the Lower Sixth, which I had regarded as a gap year following the exertions of achieving a stunning School Certificate with 1 distinction, 2 credits, 4 passes, 2 fails, I was surprised to learn from my father that my presence at Eltham College was no longer required. It seems that on reviewing my end-of-term exam results the Headmaster was not impressed with 12% average for maths, chemistry and physics, thus prompting the phone call suggesting that I was wasting the school's time and my father's money. In effect the Headmaster threw me out. Let's not pussyfoot about. I was ejected, banished, excommunicated from the school I loved and had enjoyed, for the most part, over a period of seven years from 1942.

What was I to do? At the school's career panel comprising the Headmaster (Classics) and the English master (English) I was advised not to take up engineering as my maths was poor; but then so were all the other subjects apart from art and woodwork. They had forgotten that at the age of thirteen I had been awarded the form maths prize (*Three Men In A Boat*) by the lovely Mrs. Cooper and had not twigged that my maths skills were merely lying dormant.

My father, who was ever my wise counsel, suggested that I might like to apply for an engineering apprenticeship as I had at some time expressed vague interest in automobile design. He contacted a number of firms in the South East including Vickers Armstrong

Ltd in Crayford, Kent. They did not offer me an apprenticeship as I was too old at seventeen and a half; I had missed the boat. Instead they agreed to accept me for vocational training in their engineering school. Oddly enough, when reading through my father's brief jottings on his life, I noted that he carried out patent work for Vickers Armstrong before WW2. Perhaps the name came to mind during his phone-round in his attempt to get his son launched on the commercial sea.

So off to Vickers Armstrong I went to spend the long summer holiday of 1949 with other young lads learning the rudiments of engineering. We apprentices started work at 7.15 a.m. and finished at 5.15 p.m. with an hour's break. Getting up at 6.15 to catch the 6.45 train from Sidcup station came as a bit of a shock. We were paid £1.45 (£1-9s-0d) per week which I thought was pretty generous since we were not yet contributing to the economy of the company.

The first task was to turn an old hand bastard file into a scraper (the term 'hand bastard' brought a snigger). This was done by heating the file in a furnace and allowing it to cool so as to soften it. The serrations were filed off, so we learnt the correct filing procedure. The end of the file was heated and splayed by hammering on an anvil. What an evocative object the anvil is; the farrier's main-stay, a musical instrument (the Anvil Chorus), the roadside symbol from which one anticipates a craft centre full of busy artisans, a Gretna Green artefact over which to marry, to name but a few. I have one which is mounted on a truncated trunk in my small workshop, having been banned from making it a feature in the sitting room. Back to the scraper. The splayed end was shaped on a grindstone and finally hardened and tempered once again by heating and plunging it into cold water. There was a gratifying hiss at the moment of dousing.

Next the centre lathe—what a joy to use. It produced pretty

streams of steel spirals (swarf), quite useless except for recycling. With it came magical new words such as 'headstock', 'tailstock' and best of all 'knurling'. I like the word 'knurling' as it sounds rather pleasant. It's a fine day, why don't we all go knurling? Knurling is a pleasing operation to perform and brings a satisfying result if carried out correctly. Knurling is simply working a cylindrical surface, e.g. the head of a screw knob, with a knurling tool to form a series of raised pimples (usually baby pyramids) - a tessellation, so that the item knurled may easily be gripped between finger and thumb. Knurling, knurling, knurling—lovely!

By the end of my time at Vickers I had learned many skills enabling me to make exciting things (!) such as tap-wrenches and die-holders. In fact we made a succession of tools, each one being used in the manufacture of the succeeding tool; such sensible planning to make something with a purpose. Some sixty-one years later I still possess a few of them (see below) which I made at the very excellent Vickers Armstrong apprentice school.

Scraper, die-holder, tap-wrench and pin vice (note the knurling).

Chapter 2

DEPTFORD

The personnel department, latterly called human resources (HR), at J. Stone & Co. (Deptford) Ltd was more sympathetic and offered me a four-year apprenticeship with six months' exemption on admiring the results of my six weeks' handiwork carried out at Vickers.

In retrospect, that phone call from the Headmaster was the first of many strokes of good fortune I have experienced during my lifetime, as it caused a dramatic leap from a tare-strewn path of indolence to a road towards work and serious study. Within the space of a few weeks I went from the company of my classroom friends to the machine shop floor, where I was to make the acquaintance of the backbone of the workforce of our country.

Having been given the old heave-ho from school, I deluded myself into thinking that the trauma of exams was behind me and that I was in a solely practical environment. Little did I realise that eighteen years of exams to achieve professional qualifications in engineering and patent law, and a BA degree in technology lay ahead. What I hadn't bargained for was that because of having passed my School Certificate, albeit rather modestly, I was considered a high flyer in my new place of work and was indentured as a 'student' apprentice which meant 'day-release'. Accordingly, along with other fellow student apprentices, I found myself going to the South East London Technical Institute (SELTI—later renamed Lewisham College) one day each week to study electrical engineering. In addition, I signed up for evening classes three nights a week.

In the subway of the station connecting the platforms at Chislehurst, Kent and in the pavement close to the offices of the famous brewery Shepherd Neame, in Faversham, well-worn cast-iron inspection covers can be seen all bearing the name 'J. Stone & Co. (Deptford) Ltd'. Sadly the company was broken up and sold off in 1968, but the name lives on in the London area at least, not only on 'manhole' covers but also on the name-plates attached to the many sewer air-vents which still stand in far-flung places such as Clapham, Bromley, Lee and Bermondsey. We all owe a debt of gratitude to associations which maintain our interest in these vents, better known as 'stink pipes' or 'stench pipes'. In this respect I have nothing but praise for the Clapham Historical Society members who keep us up to speed with their publication of 'Stink Pipe News'.

At the time I joined J. Stone & Co. their bread-and-butter lines were the manufacture and supply of railway equipment such as generators, lighting and air-conditioning apparatus. The generators were designed to be driven from the train carriage axles by pulleys and belts or by a universal shaft coupled to the end of the axle. Maintenance of equipment was also an essential part of the business. It was especially interesting when generators were brought in for reconditioning and cleaning as they were suspended beneath the carriage in close proximity to the 'rest room' waste outlets. We were in the fertilizing business!

The works were situated in Arklow Road, Deptford, S.E. London and spread over several acres in the region of the bifurcation of the railway viaducts leading respectively from London Bridge to Deptford and to New Cross. Many of the smaller workshops were located inside the arches of the viaducts. The main building now carries the sign 'Donovan' and can be seen from the train as it leaves New Cross for London Bridge.

In 1949 the factory and its workforce were reminiscent of the scene from the 1934 film 'Sing As We Go' in which Gracie Fields brokers an agreement between the management and the workers. The main gates were typically formed with spaced bars which we pressed our faces against at the end of a day's work. The factory hooter made its welcome sound at 6 p.m. The hours were 8 a.m. to 6 p.m. Monday to Thursday and 8 a.m. to 5 p.m. on Friday. We worked a forty-two-hour week which, by today's standards, seems long.

We clocked on and off at the entrance by putting our time-card into a slot in a machine which stamped the time in the appropriate space and simultaneously nibbled a piece off the edge of the card so that it would drop down further in the slot the next time and so re-register to receive a time stamp in the succeeding space. Three minutes grace was allowed; one second over resulted in the loss of a quarter of an hour's pay. Getting a mate to clock on or off would have meant big trouble, even if you could manage to slip out early without the gatekeeper seeing you.

At Stone's, my new-found companions became my mates. I was immediately among men who, four years before, had been fighting for King and Country. My supervisor had a spring attached to his leg to prevent foot-drop due to a bullet wound. An operator on the machine next to mine had been a rear-gunner who, on more than one occasion, had to bale out of his flaming bomber only to be returned to duty to repeat the experience. I was a little taken aback at the use of the vernacular in my new surroundings. One friendly charge-hand, Fred, on my enquiring if the quality of my box of drilled and tapped generator end-caps would suffice, said: "Suff-what? F*** me, you aint arf f***ing posh"! I was in a new world with real people. He called me Matt and was extremely tolerant of his fresh charge despite the number of screw-cutting taps I snapped when forming threads in copper commutator segments. Beastly stuff to machine, copper.

Drilling mild steel was no problem, provided you used plenty of soup, as they called the lubricating and cooling oil.

He asked what my interests were and on learning that I regularly attended church was attentive enough to follow my philosophical deliberations on the soul of man. He deflated this somewhat lofty mini-lecture with the rejoinder: "I've only got one soul and that's my arse-'ole", which took me back a little.

As to his enquiry regarding what I intended to do after completion of my apprenticeship, I said, unwittingly and rather pompously, that I would like to become a 'professional'. He paused briefly and commented "I'm a professional, mate—a professional driller". Quite so. One of many lessons from that fish pool of humanity in which I was learning to swim.

On my first day at Stone's Fred asked if I had brought a mug with me; I had remembered the overalls but no mug. He went off to search in his locker and found a battered enamel mug, thick with tea stains, and handed it to me with a cheery "This'll do!" Yuck! The canteen tea lady turned up with her tea trolley during a session of music which was played over the Tannoy for half an hour morning and afternoon. The music was broadcast by the BBC under the title 'Music While You Work'; the programme having been introduced during WW2 to encourage munition workers to greater exertion (no vocals in case of distraction). Troise and his Mandoliers formed in 1932, the year I was born, were very popular. I stared in disbelief at the liquid which frothed from the tea urn; it didn't resemble the tea my mother made. There was a thick layer of foam floating on the surface which hid the true colour, the grey side of brown. The other machinists joked that bromide had been stirred in which they said was used by the army caterers during the war to dull the soldiers' sexual urges. Whatever the truth of this, the taste was indescribable and it put me off courting for quite some time.

The rate-fixers, who were not entirely popular as they represented the management, came to the machine shop at regular intervals. They checked the piece-work rates and as a consequence I mistakenly thought I had to impress them and set about drilling as many boxes of parts as possible by clocking up double time and hence, as I thought, double pay. I was gently taken aside to be informed that I was not helping the cause of other workers, some of whom were hard put to meet the fixed time as they had complicated items to machine.

The training at J. Stone & Co. had been organised into three- or six-monthly periods working in areas including the machine shop (capstan and centre lathes, horizontal and vertical milling machines, and radial drills), armature winders, assembly shops and the steam turbo-generator test arm. The large machine shop where I worked for the first six months of my time at Stone's had a vast

GFM and Peter Cole at the back learning the essentials

array of machines. Names like Ward, Alfred Herbert, Churchill and Cincinnati come to mind. There were lines of capstan and centre lathes which were driven by endless belts from a lay-shaft mounted in plummer-blocks fifteen feet up along one wall. The noise was deafening as the metal connectors on the belts clacked each time they passed around the drive pulleys. Guards? You must be joking! This was 1949. Health and Safety—pish! Some machines had guards in the most vulnerable places but plenty of areas were left exposed for all sorts of nasty things to happen. Lurid tales were put about such as the one concerning a poor woman whose hair was caught by a swiftly revolving mandrel.

Chapter 3

CHARLTON

The Stone's foundry was located in Anchor & Hope Lane, Charlton (close to Charlton Athletic football ground, 'The Valley') where I spent time in the light metal foundry amid the choking sulphurous fumes billowing out of ladles of molten magnesium. Good

Light metal foundry with fumes

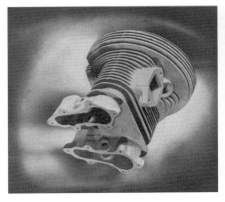

Motorcycle light alloy cylinder   Chemical analysis of metals

experience but not too helpful to my asthma. I learnt how to make sand cores which are placed in the moulds prior to pouring the metal to make holes in the final casting once the sand has been knocked out. One type of core looked like a Viking helmet as it had a pair of horns with hard metal rings at the point where the horns joined the body contiguously. I discovered that the horns formed the inlet and exhaust passages of a Matchless or AJS motorbike cylinder, the rings being embedded in the resulting casting to serve as the valve seats. Some cores had metal 'chills' embedded in them which acted as heat sinks so that different parts of the casting cooled at different rates to offset distortion or porosity.

Following a few months in the chemistry laboratory analysing, by chemical means, the composition of the bronze used in the casting of ships' propellers, I moved to the metallurgy department where I was assistant to the metallurgists and, more importantly, wore a white lab coat.

The ships' propellers made in the large foundry at Charlton were massive. Most propellers were of the four-bladed variety having a central boss and looked in like an enormous four-leaf clover. The propellers for the Cunard liners Queen Mary and Queen Elizabeth, built in the thirties, were cast at Charlton. Each propeller weighed about 60 tonnes after casting. After machining and a final finishing in the chipping shop, the net weight was about 33 tonnes.

Following several weeks of careful preparation of the mould, casting the propeller was was carried out with due ceremony. It was a dramatic event. As an assistant to the metallurgist I was given the vital job of checking the temperature of the molten bronze in the ladle prior to pouring. So off I went into the foundry with a pyrometer, which consisted of a metal probe connected by an electric cable to a meter graduated in degrees centigrade. Having noted the temperature (around 1000°C—hot!), I proceeded to the next task which was to check that the amalgam was of the correct composition. So I had to take a sample of the molten metal with a hand ladle and pour it into a small mould, allow the metal to set, cut it up and polish it and present it to the metallurgist who inspected it under a microscope to determine the relative phases of the constituent metals. If he thought the molten bronze needed a couple of extra 'cakes' of zinc, I was instructed to pass a message to the chaps on the foundry floor. Once all conditions had been satisfied pouring took place, the foundryman slowly turning the hand wheel to tip the ladle to pour the glowing metal into a header-box mounted on top of the mould. From the header-box the metal flowed down a vertical feed bore leading to a blade cavity and from there into the boss cavity and the other three blade cavities, each of which had at its tip a vertical vent (riser). Health and safety matters, again, were none too strict. I recall standing on the huge mould leaning over what would become the propeller boss as the fumes belched out of the risers.

A few days later the mould was broken up to reveal a very mucky rough cast propeller having vertical rods at the tips of the blades formed by the metal which had solidified in the risers and feed bore. The unwanted rods were trimmed off and the casting transferred to a machine shop for boring the hole which would eventually be engaged by the ship's propeller shaft. Finishing took place in the chipping shop where the 'chippers' used pneumatic chisels and templates to ensure the surfaces of the propeller blades conformed to the required helix. One didn't linger for long when passing through the chipping shop as the noise was painfully loud even with fingers firmly pressed in the ears.

The result was a magnificent shiny bronze sculpture, a work of art for which the designers, foundrymen and machinists could be justly proud.

Ship's propeller being cast. (GFM in white lab coat at the rear facing the camera). Note no guard, no hard hat, no goggles!

Chapter 4

TO CRAYFORD AGAIN

In addition to J. Stone & Co. (Deptford) Ltd and J. Stone & Co. (Charlton) Ltd the Stone's group comprised several companies such as Stone Platt, Stone Chance and a small company based in Crayford called Jones & Kent where I was seconded for several months to assemble electrical couplings; the ones having heavy cables which can be seen looped between the adjacent ends of train carriages. It was a small enterprise with no more than a dozen employees and a manager who came in at 9 a.m. The rest of us, including several apprentices, were supposed to start at 8 a.m., but having clocked in, spent the following hour huddled together warming ourselves by the stove of the kind seen in Charlie Chaplin's film 'The Gold Rush'. The stove had a chimney pipe which passed through a hole in the corrugated roof and was topped by a little coolie hat.

Having started my training at Crayford, here I was, once again by coincidence, a few hundred yards from Vickers Armstrong. I commuted between Sidcup and Crayford by rail. For some reason, which to this day I cannot attribute an explanation other than to a moment of madness, I attempted one morning to dodge paying the fare. The attempt was not at all well planned nor well executed. I got off the train at Crayford at 8.45 a.m. and handed in half a ticket; tickets in those days having the outward and inward journey details on the unitary ticket. Not only was the ticket-half the wrong colour, it had the wrong destination, the wrong date and a large W indicating a cheaper ticket for workman who travelled before 8 a.m. They did better than that in Colditz! The ticket stood out like a sore thumb and was immediately noticed by the eagle-eyed ticket collector who called me back for questioning. I feigned innocence and mumbled something about losing the correct ticket and oh how sorry I was and it was all a terrible mistake. An interview took place in the stationmaster's office and I gave my name and address, well my name at least. I was given to understand that I was to expect a summons. Gulch! Prison or a remand centre at least.

I arrived in the workshop at my usual prompt time of 8.45 a.m. and discussed the problem with my workmates and a cunning plan was hatched. One lent me his bike. I cycled at breakneck speed the five miles back to Sidcup station, purchased a valid ticket, cycled back to Crayford at breakneck speed, spoke to the ticket collector and explained, silly me, I had it in my pocket all the time, the wretched half having slipped through a hole in my jacket pocket lining, the latter having been untimely ripp'd of course, thus demonstrating where the illusive ticket had secreted itself. I deserved an ASBO had they given them in those days but with a stay of execution for sheer ingenuity and effrontery

Chapter 5

FELLOW WORKERS

During my six years at Stone's I made the acquaintance of so many marvellous people from all walks of life. One fellow student apprentice came fresh from Christ's Hospital where the boys wear gowns and yellow socks. He spoke posh, played squash at Dolphin Square and went to Humphrey Lyttleton's in Oxford Street; Humph must have been in his twenties at that time.

I met a foundryman in the light metal foundry who was proud to be a capitalist and had helped his two daughters to buy their houses. He had always voted Conservative and considered that his workmates didn't understand politics.

A turner in my section claimed that he took more than thirty aspirins per day; his skin was transparent. He looked like a character out of a Dickens film.

We received our pay in thick brown paper packets, the ones with little holes to see the coins and cut-away portions through which poked the corners of pound notes so that the money could be checked before opening. For me there was only a single pound note, as my pay for a week's work when I started was £1.75 (£1-15s-0d) of which 25p (five shillings) I generously gave to my mother for food, washing and rent. One Christmas, on receiving our pay packets, I was surprised to find a West Indian labourer, having torn open his envelope, excitedly soaking the notes one by one under the cold tap in the washroom and yelling with a flash of gold teeth: "This is hot money, man!" I didn't quite understand this activity except that the pay may have been more than usual due to extra money for two days' holiday and some overtime.

Following the machine shop I was moved to the coil winders where I met a number of tough ladies working a row of winding machines somewhat reminiscent of cotton mills. The ladies told each other naughty stories and giggled. This was a new experience which contributed to my accelerating maturity. At each winding station insulated wire ran off a large spool and on to a coil former which was rotated by an electric motor controlled by foot. The coils so made, were to be fixed on assembly in the generator yoke so that, as current is passed through them they produce a magnetic field, which induces electromotive force into the windings of the rotating armature. Simple, but not so until Michael Faraday developed his experiments on electromagnetic inductance.

One shop foreman was quite demanding and expected a very high standard from his apprentices. I spent sixteen weeks under Mr. Walter Hollage assembling brush gear. These comprised a housing containing a roller bearing and a set of four brush arms for supporting brush boxes with carbon brushes, the latter serving to pick up electricity from the armature commutator (made up of the copper segments which you will remember I had already machined elsewhere). The thing looked like an Orson Welles spaceship with four legs.

By now it will be realised that the apprenticeship was so organised that the student worked on all the components of an electric generator ending with the assembly shop. As the generator was assembled it was a pleasant surprise to recognise the various parts we had worked on in earlier stages and accordingly to have been involved in its entire manufacture.

I stayed on at Stone's an extra two years beyond the period of my original indenture to gain more experience in the drawing office supervised by Bill Cole and in the electrical experimental laboratory as assistant to Arthur Hammond.

Arthur Hammond front row left, Daphne Hemingway next to Arthur, Cynthia Hammond behind Daphne and GFM second from right second row

I found the work in the drawing office to be most stimulating and enjoyed the company of the professional draughtsmen, all delightful people. Bill Cole, or I should say Mr. Cole as he was chief draughtsman, gave me good training which enabled me to produce some serious stuff on the drawing board. As an example, the reduced drawing (below) shows a portion of an end-of-axle drive layout which I drew following an order from the Finnish railways. The layout was assembled from a heap of detail drawings of the generator (Model 22L), propeller shaft, gear-box and adaptor for mounting the gear-box to be driven by the carriage axle.

Of the draughtsmen in my section, Bill Tozer was a keen walker who invited me to join him and his two friends Ron and Michael on a tour of North Wales, where I was introduced to the splendours of Bala, Dolgelly (now Dolgellau), Capel Curig, Betws-y-Coed and Snowdon with its Pyg Track which we took in our stride. Caernarfon Castle shrouded in mist was spectacular especially at five o'clock on the morning of our arrival by night train.

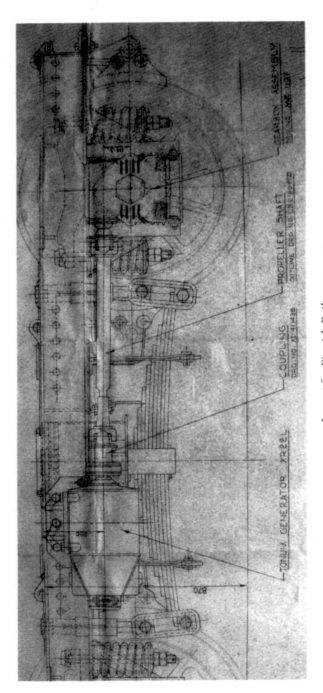

Layout for Finnish Railways

Eric White whistled themes from Beethoven's symphonies. At times I whistled with him and watched him stiffen when I deliberately pitched just under the note.

Vernon Deadman was a train enthusiast. His drawing board was near the window which looked out onto the railway viaduct and Metropolitan tube line. His name suited his passion if we think of the train driver's cab with its Deadman's Handle.

Bill Tozer

Bill, Ron & Mike

On Snowdon

Geoff Pegg told me that his family name was originally Pigg which his father changed by deed poll for some reason.

John Parker was a Norton enthusiast who convinced me that there was nothing to match the 'Featherbed' frame of a Norton motorbike. He bought his bikes from Harold Daniels of Forest Hill. At that time Geoff Duke had many Isle of Man TT successes on his Manx machine.

Christmas 1953—left to right—GFM, Bill Tozer, Ray Morris, Vernon Deadman, Mr. Cole, John Parker, Eric White, Geoff Pegg and M. R. Green.

Chapter 6

POOP, POOP!

I bought my first Norton from John and I am still not sure if he was complicit in making me look a complete biking maniac. Some jolly joker had drawn very skilfully a skull and crossbones embellished with radiating zigzags of lightening and had stuck it on the front of my helmet with Cow gum. As my goggles (Mark 8s—the type Spitfire pilots wore) were stowed on my helmet the Hell's Angels motif could not be seen until the helmet was worn, the motif being exposed after the goggles had been pulled down over the eyes. I was yelled at by a motorist as I skidded on a wet road: "You'll kill yourself, you idiot!" I was most offended. His approbation could have been brought on by the fearsome motif which I discovered later or possibly because of the ten yard two-wheel skid at right angles to the flow of traffic.

The motorcyclists I shake a fist at nowadays are no worse than I was when driving around the streets of south-east London. It was nothing to leave at 1 p.m., drive like a lunatic to New Eltham to meet my girlfriend (later my wife), have lunch at the Tudor café, roar back to Deptford to be at my drawing board by 2 p.m.

The Norton ES2

Chapter 7

MAD BIKERS

In August 1954 I teamed up with Michael Ibbetson, another student apprentice, who rode a twin-cylinder Norton Dominator 88. He was also a lunatic rider but drove skilfully with an upright riding position—no crouching over the petrol tank for him. Michael and I, both unattached 22 year olds, agreed that a tour on our motor bikes would be exciting and a lot of fun. We were not to be disappointed. Our Nortons were tuned up and panniers stuffed with the necessities to last us fourteen days, such vital things as sleeping bags and, would you believe, our navy blue blazers adorned with our respective minor public school wire-embroidered crests!

After a stop-over somewhere near Paris, we took the *Route National direction au sud* and clocked up 450 miles on our second day. We knew that we had arrived in the south of France as we passed from a cloud-covered sky to all blue, a distinct demarcation, accompanied by a sudden increase in temperature. We pitched our tent in a field next to a peach orchard and threw ourselves exhausted into our sleeping bags.

The following morning was bright and warm, bees were humming, crickets cricketing and something was making a distinctive peep-peeping sound new to our ears which we learnt was made by cigales, so camouflaged they could only be seen once your head was a mere few inches away from the insects. Michael crawled out of the tent and returned a few minutes later with some peaches; "Windfalls!", he said. Like kisses, stolen fruit tastes the sweetest.

Our tour took us to the Côte d'Azur, my first view of the Mediterranean, where we booked in for a couple of days at the youth

Cooling down in Provence 1954

hostel in La Ciotat. We met up with some French lads who at dinner enjoyed pulling my leg after I had added my starter to my main course so as to establish my Englishness. His gesture was to put his peach into the middle of his cassoulet. All very good humoured.

We ganged together with the French to go to Cassis near Marseille where we sat on the beach and watched Le Grand Spectacle de Feux d'Artifice held once a week for the tourists. I remember a crazy discussion in our schoolboy French in which I suggested that black fireworks should be used during daylight, one French boy shrugging his shoulders in typical Gallic fashion and commenting "L'esprit anglais!".

To our surprise the Mediterranean sea was not very warm. Nevertheless, we snorkelled in the crystal clear water though I never did get the hang of my mask as the ping-pong ball didn't always close off the snorkel tube as intended, which caused me to swallow large quantities of sea water. Fish a few inches long were magnified by the mask to scary dimensions. We collected *oursin de mer* (or *oeuf de mer* according to Victor Hugo) from the sea bed, spiky inver-

Mike and GFM on the rocks in Sanary

tebrates with a soft orange coloured centre which can be scooped out with a lolly stick. We sat on the beach with a small heap of the things; Michael, having been to the Mediterranean before, tucked in with relish though he didn't manage to convince me.

After our first experience of the delights of the French Riviera, especially Bandol and Sanary, we biked on along the corniches and weaved our way through the tunnels in prominences along the coast. We stopped for lunch in Nice and strolled along the Promenade des Anglais taking in the atmosphere. In Monte Carlo we didn't attempt to break the bank but instead ambled along the marina promenade and gazed at the palatial yachts, some the size of cross-channel ferries.

The customs at the French-Italian border impressed us with their flags and the total absence of any uniform. We wound our way through the Alpes Maritimes contemptuously and roared on towards Turin where we tracked down the nearest youth hostel with the help of the polizia. Mercifully we found the sole Italian policeman who could understand our version of the French language.

Having found a cosy bed for the night, the one sentence in Italian I had learnt from Hugo's phrasebook for asking for permission to camp, i.e. 'E permesso il campeggio in questa zona', became entirely redundant but never forgotten.

From Turin we headed for the Hotel Bären in Wilderswil near Interlaken where I had stayed with the School Travel Club in 1949. We stopped to admire the beautiful Lake Maggiore and pressed on to tackle the Simplon pass which took us over into Switzerland. Before reaching the summit we stopped to look back at the many hairpin bends we had travelled up, every bend being taken with an ear nearly scraping the tarmac. That was our first real taste of difficult motorcycling, further seriously hairy bends being encountered at the Grimsel and Furka passes. The Norton motorcycle was well known for its road holding and armed with this knowledge we tested our machines to the limit.

Frau Zurschmiede, the hotel owner, seemed a little disconcerted when two filthy bikers arrived in reception asking for rooms for the night. She regretted that the hotel was full; there was no room at the inn. Putting on my best hang-dog expression, I explained that I had stayed at the hotel a mere five years before with the School party led by Messrs. McIver, Slader and Buchanan. The mention of Eltham College and dropping the names of my old masters had caused Frau Zurschmiede's face to change into a huge beam of recognition; even so, there were still no rooms available but seeing how travel weary we were offered us an extra king size double bed situated on a balcony under a large overhanging eave so typical of Swiss chalets. We would sleep *en plein air* beneath the stars and in full view of the mighty Jungfrau.

After a showering, Michael and I transformed ourselves into respectable young gents by donning our oddly pannier-creased trousers, shirts and ties, and of course our badged blazers. We dined like lords and remembered to use our linen napkins, delicately wiping the corners of our mouths after each dainty mouthful. What grand fellows we were!

We ended our tour in Paris, arriving unannounced at the apartment of my pen friend's family. I first stayed there when I was fifteen for the purpose of working up my French School Certificate oral exam and knew I could rely on Madame Houssard to take us in. We slept in our sleeping bags on the floor of her elegant lounge surrounded by tasteful Louis something-or-other furniture and Limoges china.

The following morning we arranged to visit Michael's family friend, Madame Farcaux. Out came the blazers once more and off we went by Metro to another arrondissement having similarly elegant apartments. Madame Farcaux greeted us like lost sons and provided us with tea and petits fours which we balanced on our napkin-covered knees. This was indeed exceeding posh. She spoke high French which she enunciated clearly and with care-ful-ly chosen words, with which our limited vocabulary could cope, whilst encouraging our responses by sympathetically shepherding the completion of our sentences. We were actually conversing freely in French, we thought.

Our tour of France, Italy and Switzerland was taken at full throttle and by great good fortune we had only one accident on our 2000-mile trip and that was when I went into the back of Michael's machine at about 5 mph. He had braked at a fork in the road without signalling and I was too close resulting in a slight bump on his carrier. We left our sole dispute unresolved to this day!

Chapter 8

WISE COUNSEL

Twenty-first birthday parties back in the fifties involved the whole family, one's friends, parents' friends and the odd aunt thrown in for good measure. In the twenty-first century the party is generally exclusively for the birthday girl's or boy's peer group. I was fortunate because among my parents invitees was Sydney Slaughter, a patent attorney colleague and close friend of my parents. He took me aside to ask what career I intended to pursue. My mumbled reply suggested that I hadn't much of an idea and in any event it was my party and there were young ladies to attend to. I said I was anxious about all those long words used in patents. Sydney assured me that long words were not essential for describing inventions and convinced me that I would be perfectly capable of qualifying as a patent attorney with hard work. So the die was cast—*jacta alea est* as Suetonius muttered to Julius Caesar as they crossed the Rubicon!

My father Stanley qualified as a patent agent (latterly called patent attorney) in 1928 at the ripe old age of twenty-one, probably the youngest to qualify as a patent attorney. In 1951 he purchased the practice of Herbert Haddan & Co. and renamed it Matthews, Haddan & Co. It was to this firm I was articled in 1955 and was introduced to the world of intellectual property (IP).

It is always a pleasure when I meet someone who is at ease working with his father. Both Colin the plumber and Graham the roofer of happy acquaintance have been trained by and work with their fathers. I too was trained by my father in the gentlest of possible ways. He was patience personified. Each patent specification includes a detailed technical description and explanation of how

Stanley Matthews (Mr. not Sir)

the invention works. My first draft specification afforded many possibilities for improvement I'm sure, but he made a few suggestions for change without savaging my prose. The invention could well have been a simple snap-on plastic cap for the United Glass Bottle Company; turbo-fan bypass jet engines and synthetic diamonds for International General Electric came a little later.

IP broadly covers the protection given by patents, trade marks, designs and copyright. There is also the common law of 'passing-off' which is the naughtiness of passing off your goods as those of someone else. I shall confine my jottings to the areas of patents, designs and trade marks.

A patent is a monopoly granted by the Crown giving the patentee the sole right to make, use, exercise and sell the invention for a period of 20 years in the UK. No-one may, without permission, make the patented article even for private use. The patentee can institute an action for infringement and, if successful, obtain an injunction with damages, costs and delivery up of stock held by the infringer.

Whereas patents are for inventions relating to developments of mechanical, electronic, and electrical devices, drugs, chemicals, chemical processes (even plants and stem cells), design registrations are for things having shapes or patterns. For example a coffee pot being well known in itself, could well have protection as a design if it were shaped in a novel way, say in the form of a cat's head, provided of course the cat's head is distinctively different from all other existing cat's head-shaped coffee pots.

Anyone seriously interested in the niceties of design registration, if I can call it that in the event of what is to follow, may refer to the case of Vernon & Co. (Pulp Products) Ltd vs. Universal Pulp Containers Ltd (Fleet Street Reports 1980). The following is quoted verbatim:

'Vernon's manufactured bed-pans made of treated paper pulp. Vernon's sought to restrain Universal from manufacturing and selling bed-pans identical... to Vernon's. Universal brought a cross-motion to restrain Vernon's...Vernon's claims to relief...The vice chancellor dismissed both the motion and the cross-motion'. (Further observations on this would be unnecessary.)

A Trade mark is more or less what the name implies, that is a mark or logo used to indicate a connection in the course of trade between the goods being sold and the person having the right to use the mark.

The Trade Mark Register is divided into many classes covering goods and services so if you wish to market window cleaning equipment under a certain logo it may be desirable additionally to protect the logo in respect of the service of window cleaning by a service registration. We are all familiar with registered trade marks like Coca Cola, Bisto (even Ah-Bisto) and the Bass red triangle, the latter having the distinction of being Trade Mark Registration No. 1. Our firm registered many trade marks for the sweet manufacturer Trebor Ltd e.g., TREBOR, REFRESHERS and 'SHARP'S THE WORD FOR TOFFEE' and parrot logo, TREBOR EXTRA STRONG MINTS, all being household names.

The Trade Marks Act does not allow registration of descriptive marks except in special cases where the mark has become well-known by long and heavy use. The mark MINI clearly means small but, in view of heavy use, became distinctive in relation to cars and was successfully registered in respect of motor vehicles. Also registration is refused if offensive or obscene. An application to register POSTMAN in respect of dog food was understandably refused. I believe someone tried to register BAMBI for venison burgers but was turned down on grounds of poor taste (of the connotation, not necessarily of the burgers).

The origin of the Rubber Duck logo adopted by my long-standing client and acquaintance for his electronics consulting business R.B.D.K. (Electric) Ltd is rather nice, I think. Dr. Bryan Knight, an expert in electrical measurement, heard his daughter, who had just learnt her alphabet, pronouncing the letters of his initials phonetically. Try it out for yourself and speed up. Sweet isn't it.

Marks we registered for Robertson & Woodcock

Chapter 9

COVENT GARDEN

In September 1955 I joined my father in his office in Bedford Street, a stone's throw from Chancery Lane. My room looked out on the churchyard of St. Paul's Covent Garden which is known as the actors' church. The portico at the rear of the church is generally regarded to be the location for the opening scene of Bernard Shaw's play Pygmalion. The adjacent public loo is said to have the remains of the ovens used for the gruesome task of disposing of the bodies of those who died in the Plague.

St. Paul's Covent Garden & churchyard

I was taken to the Patent Office in Southampton Buildings just off Chancery Lane opposite the London Silver Vaults, a labyrinth of boutiques down in the bowels, all stuffed with items of silver from floor to ceiling. The Patent Office library houses many thousands of British and foreign patent specifications, technical publications and

British Patent Office Library Built in 1902

drawers full of indexes which I and full-time professional searchers spent many a long day trawling through and listing numbers of patents which might be relevant to a client's invention. The library, an impressive 'galleria' style construction is preserved but is no longer open to the public. The Patent Office Library, as such, is now under the aegis of the British Library and has been re-named the National Library of Science and Invention.

I learnt the art of drafting patent specifications which involve detailed technical descriptions. I use the term art because the set of claims which are the parts of the specification which define the monopoly of the invention, need careful crafting. The description of the particular example of the invention must be meticulously explained step by step.

Much of the work involved re-drafting or revising specifications which have been translated. Far from being critical of those whose first language is not English, I have unending admiration for them since apart from a reasonable command, if that be the word, of French for discussing the state of my health or the weather, some two-dozen words of German, two words in Polish and one sentence in Italian, my linguistic ability is rather limited. Nevertheless, I would be failing the world's readers if I were not to publish some gems of translations which have come to hand during the many years of revising the work sent to me by associates from foreign parts.

I shall start with the Caddie Bag Stretcher invention received from Thailand. The patent specification starts with an explanation of the difficulty to be overcome by the invention which relates especially '... to a caddie bag stretcher, while putting down the caddie bag, the standing legs of the stretcher will stretch automatically, and while lifting the caddie bag off the ground, the standing legs of the stretcher will recover automatically.' So far so good. To continue: 'The exercise of golf is very well to people who doing his work the whole day in his office. This is because the golf playing yard are all very wide and are green in colour. In there, people can breathe the fresh air, take exercise and relaxation... in playing golf, people has to choose the golf club suit to the situation of the place where the golf dropped down... Therefore... people has to bring the caddie bag from place to place, and put down the caddie bag on the place he is playing. But if no walls or trees to support the caddie bag, the caddie bag will lay down and let the clubs slide out of the bag. To prevent this, in generally, the player always hire a boy or a woman to bring the caddie bag from place to place. This is a waste to the player.' Whilst this is somewhat unusual English it is perfectly comprehensible and has a certain charm. Note that the draftsperson didn't consider that a man would have to be hired!

In a Japanese originating specification concerning ink jet printing machines, I found a lovely expression which read: '... an object is to provide... an apparatus which can exhibit a stable cleaning effect...' In another we find: 'a rim provided on its periphery with elastically deformable dogs...' An invention to do with a photocopier meets the problem that due to shorter fibres, recycled sheets of copier paper '... are apt to become nappy and generate powder.' A device for controlling the jets in an ink-jet printer may have 'a cap member arranged capably...' In a method of manufacturing semiconductor wafers use is made of a 'rough-motion stage which is driven by an inchworm...' A 'one-eyed camera' was clearly a single lens reflex camera (SLR).

Forgive me, but here's another jolly good effort by someone whose English is not quite up to speed to satisfy an examiner though nevertheless is reasonably understandable. It is quoted verbatim:

'This invention relates to a life vest which will enable people floats on the water. So far as people knows, the vast majority of today's life vests are filled with air, and the bodies of the life vest are made by rubber or other kinds of soft materials. Thus enable the life vest to produce the buoyance. But this kind of the life vest always, produce cracks and let the air leaks out of the life vest completely. Therefore, the user's life becomes not absolutely sure. To avoid the above mentioned circumstance, the life vest with the cork as the buoyage had improved, but the corks are always large in volume, and this will makes people uncomfortable or inconvenient in action.

It is an object of the present invention to provide a life vest. In using this invention, although there are cracks on it, the buoyant materials will still be hold in the body. Therefore, the safty of the user's life will be assured.' I could not have put it better myself!

Continuing on the theme of language and semantics, it is quite amazing how patent jargon can subvert normal sensible language. However, one discovers by experience that, as in most disciplines, a kind of shorthand is adopted, a code decipherable only to those in the know, in the present case in the exclusive world of patents. Here are some examples. Instead of 'little gaps' between the threads of cloth we say 'interstices' and in preference to 'a number of' we are apt to say 'a plurality' and so forth. Apart from the codification aspect, cynics may say that it serves as a device for justifying the fee imposed upon the unsuspecting lay client who discovers that his novel fish hook is, after all, 'a bifurcated elongate filamental element having integrally formed therewith a head portion of larger overall average cross section than that of said element'. More succinctly, of course, a bent pin.

Every patent specification includes a set of what are called patent claims ('revendications' in French and 'Ansprüche' in German) which serve to define the scope of the monopoly the inventor seeks to protect. The independent claim, usually the first claim of the set, is broad in scope. In other words the inventor, or more appropriately his patent attorney, sets out a list of features in the broad claim which in combination makes the magic trick work. Put simply, he (and yes of course *she*) is telling the world what they must not do and anyone copying the idea with all the features of the broad claim will infringe and down the copier must go! The infringer should expect a visit from the 'boys' which would take the form of a letter from the patentee's attorney firing a shot across the bows or a writ from solicitors. The story is told that in Hong Kong the 'boys', *aka* the police, dealt severely with the infringers who received a beating with batons and had their goods confiscated. So far, to my knowledge, such extreme handling of a patent infringer hasn't yet happened in the UK.

Trouble starts when the alleged infringer asserts in his defence that one of the features of the claim is missing from his device. The omission of one feature should put the infringer in the clear. But nothing is so simple of course. Now we are in the field of 'interpretation'. Many battles have been fought in the courts over whether or not the alleged infringing product falls within the patent claims. The copier may have omitted a feature which has been included in the broad claim but he comes unstuck if the patentee can establish with evidence that the feature was *inessential* and that the real nub of the invention lay in other features in combination. To support the assertion that the feature is inessential requires evidence and this is usually obtained by bringing in expert witnesses. The whole process becomes complicated and, not unsurprisingly, expensive.

As an indication of how involved a patent action can become I shall now recount the story as it happened some years ago when I was in practice with my father and brother. Fortunately the technology in not too sophisticated and neither was the client! Read on...

Chapter 10

THE "WORKMATE" WORKBENCH

On reflection it would have been better to have been out of the office the day Mr. Andrews sought my firm's assistance. It wasn't so much his plight in having received a 'thing' from Mr. Hickman's solicitors which concerned me, but my lack of conviction as to the accuracy of the background history of his lamentable situation.

For no reason other than being confronted by his hirsute, but otherwise bare chest, did I have a sense of ill ease as the new client sat before me—though I have to admit that my misgivings were influenced by his rather short shorts and open-toed sandals, apparently necessitated by an exceptionally hot summer's day. The bare chestedness was distracting and I can remember thinking, as I sat there gently perspiring in my chalk-striped all-wool suit with waistcoat suitably embellished with my grandfather's Albert watch chain thus adding sobriety to the interview, that the situation was unusual.

It transpired that the gist of the writ indicated that Mr. Hickman, the inventor and patentee, was offended by Mr. Andrews' activity. The patented product (marketed under the name Workmate®), which comprised a collapsible workbench having a pair of elongate vice members with independently operable screws, had enjoyed considerable commercial success as evidenced by a Trifid-like spread of the things over the entire planet. Two legitimately purchased samples of the same, ravaged by paint and saw-cuts, reside in my garage.

The Andrews' workbench did give one more than a déjà-vu feeling about it which was not surprising since it also had all of the Workmate features. The only lifeline I could throw to Mr. Andrews was to attack the patent on the ground that it covered a product which was not new or that it was obvious, having no inventive step over what had been known before. A search at the British Patent Office library revealed a number of patented workbenches but none seemed either to anticipate the patented features or came close enough to support an argument of obviousness.

Now it so happened that for some years I have had an interest in antiquarian books to the extent that after this episode I created and ran a second-hand book-shop—but that is another story. From time to time I used the services of a bookbinder by the name of John Smart whose bookbinding business address included '...at the rear of Lewisham Way'. It occurred to me that he might be able to assist us in our time of trouble.

Mr. Smart was a charming and most interesting man to engage and was highly skilled and knowledgeable in his sphere. It was always a pleasure to visit his workshop which was located in the loft of an old coach-house. On climbing the external wooden stairs to the loft one was confronted by a sight which was evocative of craftsmanship of a bygone age. Sheets of Moroccan leather, cartridge paper, cloth and muslin lay in not so neat piles around the room along with hundreds of books, ancient and modern (including several sets of our Reports of Patent Cases) awaiting binding or restoration. On a table lay the tools of his trade and a glue-pot in which simmered pearl bone-glue exuding an aroma familiar to those of us who at school took the now outmoded woodwork classes. Among the equipment were two or three guillotines and, not insignificantly, several laying presses of various sizes.

One larger laying press was mounted on two of the upstanding sides of an open box-like structure and for all the world looked like a workbench and at times was indeed used as such. A laying press has a pair of elongate members and a pair of independently operable screws passing through large clearance holes in one member and engaging in threaded holes in the other member. The device serves to hold the pages of a book together whilst gluing tapes to the edges. It seemed to have all the features of the patented workbench and therefore we had a good chance of invalidating the patent. With the help of counsel the Smart laying press was duly cited in the suit.

The trial had many aspects of a familiar court-room drama with the exception of a scene in which the defendant, on being pressed by a Perry Mason equivalent at the English Patent Bar, breaks down in floods of tears howling: "I did it. I infringed. He was making lots of money (*sob*) and I wanted to be a tax exile in Guernsey too." Neither was there a last minute reprieve by a 'lost' witness. Worse, the witness we did put on the stand reminded one of a Boulting Brothers comedy when he uttered the immortal words: "Not a word of a lie, yer Lordship." as he wagged his finger at the bench. At this, eyes rolled and wigs slipped over the brows of defending counsel.

Mr. Justice Graham was of the opinion that the laying press was not a workbench on a reasonable interpretation of the wording of the patent, with the result that Mr. Andrews lost his case along with his shirt—not for the first time, one recalls.

I noted from the law report of this case that the judge was very gracious in his comments: 'I am not saying that either of them [the defendant and the witness] is deliberately misleading the Court as to the true facts…' Nicely put I think.

Aside from the matter of the interpretation of the patent, the construction of the infringing product and the presence of about twenty workbenches showing the progressive modification and development of the invention since its conception, the strongest support for the patent in my view was the well-rehearsed casual erection of a more than life-size photograph of the Duke of Edinburgh presenting the Queen's Award to Industry to Mr. Hickman for his

Workmate! We couldn't possibly have matched that.

To add insult to injury, Mr. Andrews magically disappeared leaving no forwarding address and no payment of our bill. As was famously stated by Terry Jones, in the Monty Python film 'Life of Brian': 'He's a very naughty boy!'

Chapter 11

FALKLANDS WAR

One invention which failed to get off the ground was the destruction-proof junction box which apparently enjoyed some success in the field during the Falklands conflict in 1982. (For those in the trade I do not propose here to discuss the question of *'novelty'* in view of its temporary and secret deployment in Goose Bay). The device serves or served as an electrical connection between a mobile generator and a Rapier Missile launcher. The modified junction box, I was informed, was state of the art although there were minor technical difficulties which had to be resolved.

I was duly summoned by the client and arrived by car at the appointed time. Parking was a problem but with great skill I managed a rather smart five-point turn between the various pieces of equipment and cables stacked in the car park. The receptionist left me with a cup of coffee and returned ten minutes later to say that further technical difficulties had been encountered, this time being of a substantial nature.

An apologetic managing director eventually appeared along with a much harassed inventor who led me through the design section into the area of the car park used for equipment testing. The junction box had clearly been put through an extreme compression test or perhaps the invention lay in its strikingly noticeable two-dimensional aspect, i.e. it was squashed flat. With great effort and concentration, borne of many years' experience, I noted the inventive features and departed hastily with an acute feeling of anxiety in view of the crunching sound I had heard during my earlier parking manoeuvrings relative to the test site. Oops!

Chapter 12

M R S .   M O R R I S

It was shortly after I had qualified as a patent attorney in 1963 when Mrs. Morris came to our office to patent her latest breast pad.

"You wouldn't think I have had a bilateral would you?" said Mrs. Morris after a brief exchange of greeting. A quick glance in the direction indicated by her posture and some agile thinking on my part gave me to understand that she had undergone a double mastectomy.

Once comfortably seated in front of my desk, she explained how devastating the effect of an operation of this kind is to a woman both physically and mentally. First there is the trauma of being informed that due to the extent of the cancer tumours, the breast, or in the case of Mrs. Morris, both breasts, would have to be removed along with all the lymph nodes. Then follows the discomfort of the scar and the disablement of muscles and numbness in the underarm and back region. Post operative treatment may be given which takes place over several months and comprises chemotherapy and radiotherapy, both rather debilitating.

My client went on to explain how depressed most women felt after what is tantamount to mutilation albeit for the purpose of survival. It transpired that she was in the unique position of being able to offer her services as a hairdresser and, through the National Health Service, as a fitter of breast prostheses. Her fitting room was conveniently above the salon.

She told me about one young woman in her twenties who had had a similar operation to hers and who came to her in a very distressed state. Mrs. Morris had instructed her customer to bring her favourite bra and sweater. The make-over comprised a smart hair-do in the salon followed by a fitting in the upper room where she tucked pads into the otherwise sadly empty cups of the bra. The young woman was guided to a position before a cheval mirror and asked how she felt now. She was a different person compared to the one who had arrived an hour or so before and left with a feeling that life wasn't so bad after all.

The breast pads Mrs. Morris had made evolved just as the Workmate had evolved, one improvement followed by another. The first prototype had been simply one of Mr. Morris's handkerchiefs filled with millet seed. The reasoning behind this was that the existing breast pad was merely a machined piece of cotton material pouch stuffed with a lump of foamed rubber. Of course, there were many types of breast enhancement pads available at the time but most, as Mrs. Morris explained, were uncomfortable and did not have either a natural appearance or, more especially, did not move or feel as part of the body. Mrs. Morris's idea of the handkerchief and millet seed was to attempt to simulate the weight and movement of the natural breast. However, she experienced two problems with the millet seed which she described to me in her light-hearted way. Her dentist was alarmed, as was she, when some seed, organised, I imagine like a column of ants in a Tom & Jerry cartoon, trickled from what remained of her cleavage. The other problem was that the seed tended to sprout due to the warmth and moisture from the body. Something more permanent was called for.

The machined cotton pouch was retained but instead of seed she used small pellets of plastics material, like miniature Smarties®, which lay loosely one upon another affording the movement and softness of the normal breast. The pouch was only partially filled with the pellets so that they shifted and settled against the inside walls of the pouch which was pre-formed to the classical European breast shape which, as those who take an interest in this specialised subject will be aware, is slightly upturned and with a gentle droop. The choice of plastics material having a specific gravity more closely allied to the specific gravity of normal breast tissue was also important to the success of the invention.

Developments of Mrs. Morris's invention are available today e.g. the Bean-a-Boob marketed by Nicola Jane and other companies.

I recall how enthusiastic Mrs. Morris was when telling me with great emphasis how important it is for breast cancer survivors to receive the best psychological counselling as she was so ably placed to provide. Little did I think that my new-found expertise would be invaluable forty years later when a close friend experienced the same problem.

Chapter 13

CURIOUSER AND CURIOUSER

During my forty-eight years in the patent profession I have been fortunate enough to have made the acquaintance of many inventors, mostly I am pleased to say of a serious disposition but some whom I shall class as slightly odd—nutty even. The following inventions I describe are an assortment of ideas which I shall leave to the reader to assess as to brilliant or nutty or shades in between. The majority of our clients were serious manufacturers. However, we did have a plentiful share of small inventors, those who 'walk in off the street' as we refer to them.

The trouble with feeding a King Charles spaniel is the ears— they are long. Accordingly, when the animal feeds its ears dangle in its food dish and become gunged up with food. After each feed it is necessary to scrub the distal ends of the dog's ears, which is time consuming and a discomfort to the dog. One method of solving this problem was to gather the dog's ears from each side of its head and peg the ears together so that they rested on the top of the animal's head. This is effective, apart from being painful, but moreover looks silly and is therefore an embarrassment to the poor creature. The second method, the subject of the invention, comprised a strip of composite material having a wadding sandwiched between the facing rectilinear elongate sheets of woven cotton, each end supporting a pocket. In other words an oven cloth. The feeding problem is solved by placing the oven cloth over the dog's head with the pockets innermost and tucking the ears into the pockets. Voila!

Like Winston Churchill I have had a stab at bricklaying. Unlike the great man's wall at Chartwell, mine was a modest chimney breast. Anyone who has attempted bricklaying will appreciate the difficulties involved and not least in achieving smooth pointing without getting the mortar all over the face of the bricks. The client wished to patent his device which looked remarkably like a broken window stay which of course it was.

The above two inventions fall into the category of a new use of a known product which has been the subject of much conjecture in the patent courts for many a year. Even if a patent were granted for such a device it would be a little difficult to enforce the patentee's rights.

Of the rather quirky inventions which came across my desk was the novel bar of soap. The inventor was at pains to ensure me that I understood that considerable waste of soap occurred each day in every household. We try to use the remaining thin piece by pressing it onto the newly unwrapped bar. This attempt at saving is rarely successful. His idea was to form the soap with a hollow centre. Of course! Why hadn't it been thought of before. How he was going to manufacture such a product was not explained, but if manufacturing hollow sweets is technically possible why not soap? The advantages were explained as: i) the soap would float—low specific gravity floating soap is known but everyday soap could be used, and ii) more significantly, there would be a large saving in material because there was no material in the middle to be wasted! As the inventor couldn't provide technical support for his project he decided to wash his hands of the whole matter.

Returning to the theme of prosthetics, I was surprised to see a large hairy policeman enter my office and take a seat on the other side of my desk. He wasn't wearing his uniform so it was not until some time through the conversation did he reveal that he was in the Force, though clearly he was large and hairy. Hairy, that is, until he removed the subject of the invention.

He looked me straight in the eyes and said: "You'd never guess that I'm wearing a hairpiece would you?" Contrary to my response to Mrs. Morris, I lied in reply because I had already spotted little pieces of canvas and stitching in the region of the parting. This story reminds me of Jasper Carrot's tale of the young lady who was taken to dinner by her boyfriend, he being similarly crowned, who said that he had a secret to tell her and she replied "What's that, Wiggy?"! To explain the idea behind his novel wig construction he removed it from his head with a deft sweep of the hand, the thing making a slurping noise as he did so, and placed it on my desk blotter. I lifted it with the end of my pencil, very gingerly in case it went for me, and studied it as it swung in hypnotic fashion before my eyes. It was warm and after placing it back on the blotter it curled up like one of those coloured cellophane fish found in Christmas crackers by which, it is alleged, one can tell if a person is in love. I prepared and filed a patent application for the client but he never went ahead with it.

One strange client called without an appointment and sought my advice on his invention and confused me in his introduction by saying: "Well, I've done a bit of bird, haven't I… d'you know what I mean?" He seemed a little alarmed when I talked about *filing* and *prosecuting* an application. The details of his idea escape me.

Another called in to seek protection for his plug-hole adaptor for preventing spiders from coming up through the U-trap of the bath waste pipe thus reducing the risk of the spread of cancer caused by the malevolent arachnids. How the spiders came up through the U-trap is not clear but one imagines the creatures being kitted out with tiny goggles and flippers.

Yet another had the brilliant idea of adapting a Quality Street tin for attachment to the handlebars of a bicycle but I wasn't to let his wife know because she would be mad at him for wasting money paying our vast fees. I remember charging him eighteen guineas for drafting a specification and paying the Government application fee. He paid with musty pound notes which he said he kept under his mattress out of view from his wife.

So many ideas have been put forward for achieving 'perpetual motion'—the holy grail of inventions. One client of mine described his invention as a box with a shaft extending from it which rotated (as he said) at a constant speed, there being no input of energy. I am still waiting for the demonstration model I asked for.

My father tells the story of a 'perpetual motion' client he had when he was a newly qualified patent attorney. The inventor's sister came first to impress upon father that he was a brilliant man and if his invention seemed impossible it was to be remembered that radio was thought impossible only a few years previously. He described his idea which comprised an energy storage device for attachment to a bicycle whereby energy could be stored when going downhill for driving the machine uphill. He was assured that perpetual motion is impossible. As he insisted, father told him to go away and come back when he could demonstrate a model. Eventually he turned up with an old second-hand bicycle with a gear-box enclosed in a soldered chain-case. He would not describe what was in the gear-box but said as it had involved him in financial expenditure (ten shillings for the bicycle) and trouble to make the model, a trial at least was justified. With great reluctance and much chiacking by his colleagues leaning out of the office windows, father went with him to Sussex Street off the Strand which leads downhill towards the river. Having mounted the bike he pressed hard on the pedals which rotated with a jerky movement making it difficult to maintain balance. Ignoring the loud clanking coming from the chain-case containing the inventive features, he gathered speed while the inventor, with hair and coat flying in the wind, ran behind crying: 'Keep going, Mr. Matthews.

You're doing fine!' Eventually, exhausted, father threw down the bicycle and left his client tearing his hair in despair. *Nul points!*

Chapter 14

THE FURTIVE CLIENT

For an invention to be patentable it has to be novel and to involve an inventive step. It may be novel to have two bells on a bicycle instead of one but that's not inventive. If an invention is published by printed matter or, say, shown on television, it is fatal to the novelty aspect.

Clients are urged not to tell a soul and not to publish until a patent application covering the idea has been filed (we call it 'lodged') at the Patent Office. Added to the client's anxiety not to publish is the thought that the invention is stunningly brilliant and accordingly the world will beat a path to his door. Secrecy is very important of course but sometimes this instils an unnecessary degree of furtiveness as in the following scene recorded by my secretary.

SUE: (*Secretary answers phone*) Good afternoon, Mr. Matthews' office.
CLIENT (prospective): I want to speak to Mr. Matthews. I was recommended to you by Rayleigh Moulding.
SUE: I'm afraid he's out of the office until about 4.30. Would you like me to ask him to call you then or perhaps tomorrow?
CLIENT: What time tomorrow?
SUE: About 2.30?
CLIENT: Is that in the afternoon?
SUE: Yes. May I have your company's name and telephone number? (*Pause while client ponders*)
CLIENT: OK. It's RIP Bodies…..Oh, I think I'll call him tomorrow.
SUE: I'll tell him you rang. Goodbye.

(*4.30pm the same day*)

CLIENT: Hello, can I speak to Mr. Matthews?

SUE: I'll put you through.

CLIENT: Oh, I thought you said he wouldn't be in today.

SUE: He's just come back.

GFM: Good afternoon Mr. Davis. The matter seems urgent. Would you please let me know the gist of your idea.

(*Pause while client ponders yet again*)

CLIENT: Hmm. Can I tell you? How do I know you won't pinch my idea. A nod's as good as a wink to a blind horse.

GFM: Of course I wouldn't. I'm just like your doctor—everything is strictly confidential.

CLIENT: 'Ang on a minute. Just going to make sure the door's shut.

(*Footsteps recede, door bangs, footsteps approach*)

CLIENT: Hello.

GFM: Hello.

CLIENT: (*Sotto voce*) I want to protect an idea just like the man who done the cats eyes. Mr. Clark said you could put a thing on it.

GFM: Yes, I can file a patent application. Send me a drawing and brief description and I'll see what I can do.

CLIENT: You will keep it to yourself. Word gets around in the trade.

GFM: Of course. I'm just like your doctor…

Chapter 15

CAPITAL VENTURE

We met at Biggin Hill airport in the pouring rain. The chartered Cessna 3C had been fuelled ready for the flight to the Channel Islands. I had been asked to join the assembled company consisting of the chairman, his fellow director, a lady with a fox fur and the pilot. I was there in order to provide any advice regarding the invention which was to be marketed by the enterprise about to be registered as an off-shore company.

The Cessna took off from runway 21 and was immediately enveloped in thick cloud. We were thrown about violently due to severe turbulence. As an engineer I am well aware that the wings of an aircraft should flex but on this occasion they positively flapped. The journey to Guernsey was broken to pick up a fifth passenger at Gatwick Airport, the pilot skilfully wrestling the aircraft solely by navigational instruments to the threshold of 27.

Landing at Guernsey in fine weather, we took a taxi to St. Peter's Port where the business of registration was effected. My job was to gather information about the invention which, up to that point, was being kept a closely guarded secret. The newly registered company was to import from Sweden a very special resin constituted by a very special formula made in a very special laboratory situated in the environs of Malmö.

The special resin was to be applied to ships, more especially to the hulls of oil tankers of up to 300,000 tonnes displacement, the coating of resin affording a substantial reduction of drag with a consequential enormous saving in fuel.

The composition of the special resin enabling me to draft a

specification not being made available to me in the Channel Islands, I was detailed on our return to get on the next plane to Scandinavia. The flight and hotel in Copenhagen were duly booked in my name and off I went. As I took the early morning hydrofoil crossing to Malmö I saw myself in the rôle of a British secret agent, trench-coat with collar turned up and trilby hat with brim turned down.

I interviewed the chief chemist involved in the production of this sophisticated resin and pressed him for the specific ranges of the ingredients. As the discussion progressed, mercifully in English, it was evident that the poor man was quite non-plussed. He could not understand my questioning which was something along the lines of: 'Could you tell me which of the constituents of the resin do you think are essential to ensuring the reduction of the ship's drag?'

The chief chemist seemed to have no idea what I was talking about especially when I mentioned coating the ships' hulls and fuel saving qualities. He said his resin was *floor polish* which his company had been marketing for years. Even then I didn't twig that I was an unwitting party to a rather elaborate swindle.

This situation is known as being drawn in to add respectability to robbery. It was not until many years later that I was informed that the whole set-up together with my carefully drafted patent specification was organised to be sold as a potential money winner. Fortunately, no punter was found to dupe and the venture was sunk without trace.

Chapter 16

O N E   G O O D   T U R N

Managing a two, three or four-manual organ necessitates full employment of hands and feet. Even the most dexterous organist prefers to have an assistant in attendance to shift stops and turn pages of music on the nod of the organist.

I am proud to say that I have made a substantial contribution to a recording of Bach's Goldberg variations. The recording session took place at Eltham College and was successfully achieved despite the many flights passing over en route to Heathrow. (As I write there are no planes overhead due to the cloud of volcanic ash from Iceland). My part was to turn the pages of music while David Sanger (former pupil at Eltham) merely depressed the keys of the harpsichord in the correct sequence. Page turning is a serious business and it doesn't do to turn two pages over at a time.

David is, of course, an accomplished organist and is currently (2010–2011) President of the Royal College of Organists. Quite often he employs the services of an assistant, such as a music student, to turn pages when the music necessitates many changes of registration. To obviate the need for an organist to dragoon an assistant, Richard Graves came up with his novel page turner.

Richard was a church organist who spent many hours creating his sophisticated page turner. His apparatus comprised a series of wires, which attached by means of crocodile clips to the pages to be turned. The wires were spring-loaded and held cocked by a notched bar operated by an air piston to release the wires sequentially, the air piston being connected by a rubber tube to a motorhorn-like rubber bulb of the kind readily obtainable from chemists.

In operation, the organist, after having set up the apparatus on the organ desk and clipped the wires to the pages of music, places the operating bulb under his left or right buttock depending upon the player's preference. As the player comes to the last few bars of each right hand page all that is necessary to do is to rock the body so that the bulb is squeezed by the overlying buttock. Hey-presto, the wire is released and the page whips over so that there is no interruption for the player. There was a slight weakness in this arrangement as some music calls for repeated passages (Da Cappa).

Chapter 17

NAPPY RETURNS

They say that necessity is the mother of invention and this is true of a lady client who came to our office to seek protection for her invention. She was Valerie Hunter Gordon, the daughter of Mr. Ferranti of the famous Ferranti manufacturer of radios and electronic equipment. In view of the connection it was thought that she may be an electronics expert. How wrong we were. She had constructed a new improved plastic panty for babies. She had six young children and had become bored of stewing towelling nappies. Consequently, she designed a reusable plastic panty with a disposable nappy insert. We obtained patents and design registrations for her. Friends advised her that she was wasting her time and money and should abandon further attempts at marketing the pants. With persistence she persuaded Robinsons of Chesterfield to manufacture under licence and the plastic pants and the inserts were sold under the trade mark Paddi Pads in chemist shops all over the United Kingdom. Similar items are sold today under the mark Pampers®.

To our surprise Mrs. Hunter Gordon returned twenty-five years later with her new and further improved designs, this time brought on by the necessity of changing her grandchildren's nappies. Truly the mother of invention.

Chapter 18

IMPROVED DECAL

Transfers or decals as they are sometimes called, have been known for more than a century. The kind we used as children which necessitated floating the composite sheet in a saucer of water were great fun, especially when applying roundels as the finishing touch to a model airplane, but the cause of some concern to parents when the water migrated all over the table. My father took great care of his dining/billiard table but somehow on occasions water managed to seep through between the leaves which formed the tabletop and drip onto the baize thus incurring his displeasure. (By the way, it was this billiard table described in *'You're the doctor'* that served as my indoor air-raid shelter during WW2).

Water slide decals are generally printed face up and are attached to a paper backing sheet by a soluble layer such as dextrose corn sugar which serves the dual role of adhesive and release.

Frederick Mackenzie, a Scottish printer by profession, came to us with this idea which was to print images onto a wax release layer applied to the backing sheet. For lettering the print was applied in the normal way and on the backing sheet with rows of letters in upper and lower case according to frequency of their use i.e. plenty of letters 'a' and few of letters 'z'. The compositions of the printing ink and the release layer were empirically selected so that the printing remained in place on the release layer until detached for adhesion to the work surface.

For release and transfer Mr. Mackenzie designed a frame with a translucent gauze. The user placed the gauze over the selected letter, pressed the gauze in the region of the letter which attached itself to the underside of the gauze and remained there until the letter was placed over the appropriate position on the work surface. Positive registration was facilitated as the printed letter and intended location were clearly seen through the gauze. LETRASET had been born.

The next development Mr. Mackenzie devised enabled the frame and gauze to be dispensed with altogether. Following further adjustment of the composition of the ink, release layer and translucent backing sheet it became possible to detach a transfer by simply aligning the printed image over the target position on the work piece and applying pressure. From this innovation there was a revolution in the field of commercial art. Stickers became popular with children and dry transfers appeared in our Kellogg's cornflake packets.

It is alleged that Mr. Mackenzie sold his patents and with the proceeds crossed the water jump to pursue his ambition of selling yachts to wealthy Americans from a base in Bermuda, each time providing a personal crewing service to sail back to the United States with the proud owners.

Chapter 19

PETER & FRIENDS

Have you been fascinated, as I have, by the special effect images we see on television? How did those electronic engineers devise equipment for causing a TV picture to fracture into separate portions which, after being suspended in mid-air follow each other in spiral form and disappear as though going down a bath plug-hole? The opening credits of Barry Norman's (latterly Jonathan Ross's) film programme, include graphics in which a moving strip of film has a series of frames, each frame showing a moving picture. Clever stuff!

This now gets a little technical but bear with me and all will be revealed. We take for granted seeing a moving picture but rarely stop to think how this is produced. Cinematic pictures give moving pictures by projecting images from a succession of 'still' frames, each frame being stopped for a fraction of a second in the projection gate. If the frames are passed at 24 per second the eye (mind) is fooled into seeing a moving picture free of flutter. An inventor by the name of Friese-Green came up with the stop-frame idea which was later developed to successful cinematography by Thomas Edison.

To have some understanding of how moving pictures appear on our TV screens I find it helps to consider the destination indicator panel in train carriages. The names of the stations appear to travel from right to left but of course it's nothing of the kind. The array (or raster) of LEDs (light emitting diodes) are illuminated by electrical signals generated by a computer, the LEDs going on and off in a sequence to give the lettering the appearance of travelling along.

In much the same way, digital television screen is formed with a raster of pixels (picture elements) made up of triads (three discrete spots representing the primary colours of red, blue and green) which in combination produce a hue dependent upon the strength of the signals applied respectively to the triads. The many thousands of pixels on a TV screen are controlled by a computer, as in the indicator panel already mentioned. However, the computer is organised to produce a succession of picture frames, as in cinematography. The big break-through came with the digital frame store (DFS) which, as the name implies, is a store which can hold an entire picture frame of information in digital form.

Quantel is a company, based in the United Kingdom and founded in 1973, that designs and manufactures digital production equipment for the broadcast television, video production and motion picture industries. Headquartered in Newbury Berkshire, their 126,000 sq. ft. building was built on the 6.7 acre site where Vickers Armstrong (that name again!) manufactured Spitfire fighter aircraft during World War II. Air raid shelters are still present in the grounds of the site. The name Quantel comes from Quantised Television which alludes to the process of converting a television picture into a digital signal.

Peter Michael, the entrepreneur and a founder member of Quantel, was knighted in 1989 for services to industry. Other electronic engineers in his formidable team were Richard Taylor MD of Quantel 'the man who built Quantel and changed the face of television' as his friend and long-term Director of Research, Paul Kellar, describes him in his tribute to Richard who, sadly, died in 2009 at the age of 64. Quantel developed the first all-digital framestore (Quantel DFS 3000) which was first used in the live TV coverage of the 1976 Olympic Games held in Montreal, to generate a moving picture as an inset within a moving picture. The fluttering Olympic

Torch was seen in the insert with the remainder of the picture showing the athlete running with the torch as he entered the stadium.

In the early eighties I was invited to visit Quantel to see a demonstration of a piece of apparatus of particular interest to me as I am still pursuing the notion that one day I shall become an artist. The apparatus known as Paintbox is similar to an artist's pallet and canvas except that it is fully electronic.

The demonstration was helped by the fact that the operator was an actual artist, with appropriately long hair, who used Paintbox with great skill. The 'canvas' comprised a plain white screen except that beneath the surface plastics sheet there was arranged a raster of pixels, the colours of which could be activated by a 'brush' (stylus) carrying the 'paint colour'. An electronic pallet of 'paints' was arranged along one side of the canvas.

The artist selected a brush size, even an 'air-brush'. (A friend of mine went into an art shop and asked for an air-brush and was told to try the ladies' hair stylists next door!) The selected brush was touched on the pallet of the colour required and the brush stroked on the canvas, the coloured stroke representing the stroke of a normal brush with uncanny similarity. Even washes could be produced without the nasty runs down the paper of which every budding artist is aware. If a mixture of colours was required then two or more coloured pallets could be touched and astoundingly combined in an electronic mixing pallet.

Since this original concept, Paintbox has undergone various improvements. Many of the major films released since 1999 have been created or include image manipulation using Quantel technology; Star Wars II and III, The Lord of the Rings and the Fellowship of the Ring being familiar examples.

Video technology developed by Quantel gave rise to many of the special effects seen on television today. From 1968 to 1983, my company was responsible for obtaining patents in the United Kingdom, United States and many other countries on the stream of inventions being developed by the Quantel team. In addition to Peter, Richard and Paul, I was privileged to collaborate with other brilliant electronic engineers such as Tony Searby, Ian Walker, Peter Owen and Barry Miles. With their help my company was able to prepare the technically testing descriptions with accompanying diagrams and flow-charts necessary to satisfy the Patent Office examiners in the major manufacturing countries of the world. It was during this time that I received instructions from Quantel's in-house patent attorney, Ralph Atkinson, who was himself an electronics expert.

In 1989 Quantel won an action for infringement against Spaceward Microsystems for infringement of their Paintbox patents, the patents withstanding an attack on their validity due largely to the evidence given by Richard Taylor. I have to admit that I was greatly relieved, as no doubt were the Quantel team members, that their patents weathered the storm.

Chapter 20

WAVING THE FLAG

My father was a great believer in developing personal contacts with our associates located in all of the major countries of the world. Before WW2 he was a frequent visitor to Berlin (see '*You're The Doctor- You Decide*') where he arranged licence agreements with I.G. Farbenindustrie through his counterpart, Erich Schubert. In 1946 he went to Canada, again for patent licensing, several times to the United States by way of both Cunard liners mentioned above, and by Concorde to S.E. Asia where he established good connections with several Japanese attorneys.

We obtained patents for inventions as diverse as cameras (Franke & Heidecke in former West Germany and VEB Kamera- u. Kinowerke in Dresden, former East Germany, tobacco processing machinery (AMF Legg), contact lenses (Československá academie věd), roll-on roll-off ferries (VEB Schiffbauwerke), electronic signal processing (Quantel Ltd), semiconductors (RCA), synthetic diamond (International General Electric), some of which I shall refer to later.

Father became well known in East Germany especially after he was asked to present a paper at the State University of Humbolt, Berlin. The name of Matthews, Haddan & Co spread through East Germany like a forest fire and work came in from many VEB (**Volkseigenebetriebe**) companies such as those in Rostock, Erfurt and Dresden.

I referred before to the one-eyed camera which more correctly translates as the single lens reflex camera (SLR). Prior to the dismantling of the Berlin Wall in 1989, my company handled the inventions of VEB Kamera- u. Kinowerke Dresden who were SLR specialists. The SLR camera is easily recognised as the top of the casing has a distinguishing bulge which houses a pentaprism, an optical device which receives image light through the camera lens, reflects the light from several surfaces, two of which are at right angles to each other, and exits the image at a higher level towards the camera eye-piece.

A pivotal mirror is arranged at 45° to the optical axis of the lens and beneath the pentaprism to receive the light from the lens and direct the image towards the prism for viewing. On looking through the view finder the user sees what the objective lens sees. On camera release, hey presto, the mirror swings away from the optical axis so that the light from the image instead of reflecting from the mirror, goes directly to the camera film or, as in present-day digital cameras, to the pixel array, as soon as the shutter opens.

These SLR cameras were quite different from the cameras made by other very long-standing camera clients of ours, Franke und Heidecke, and marketed under the famous trade mark Rolleiflex. Their cameras had a viewing system separate from the camera lens in which a viewing lens projected the image of the object to be photographed onto a frosted glass screen. The two lens systems were mechanically coupled so that as you focussed the image on the viewfinder screen the image to be recorded would be focussed on the film plane ready for the moment when the shutter is operated. Clear? Of course it is! Anyway, describing the two types of camera is to justify our view that there was no conflict of interests between the two important clients, one being in the West and the other in East Germany, until the day came when Franke und Heidecke decided to market SLRs imported from Singapore.

We had to choose between the two clients as the cheeky older client asked us to stop acting for the other people. Since the

West German firm had made the change from the two-lens system to the single lens, for the sake of fairness, and having nothing to do with the fact that the communist controlled excellent payers sent us very much more work than the other lot, we chose the East Germans who, along with many other East German companies, had been loyal clients. As it happened, our agonising was irrelevant, *nihil ad rem* as we say in the trade, because the Berlin Wall came down and all the Volkseigenebetriebe companies disappeared into history.

Chapter 21

HARRY COLLETT BOLT

Mr. and Mrs. Bolt must have had a twinkle in their eye for a second time when choosing names for their baby boy following his birth on the 4th February 1910 in Timaru, Canterbury, New Zealand. Also did they, I wonder, have aspirations for their son to become an engineer.

Not only is the surname indicative of a 'securing means', a generic term we use for bolts, nails, screws and any number of fixing devices known to man, but his second given name was Collett. To explain: I know a lady of a certain age who, during the War, quality checked collets which served to grip Spitfire components when being machined on a lathe.

After serving in the Middlesex Regiment (The Duke of Cambridge's Own) during the War, Major Harry Collett Bolt set to work to design portable and *intentionally* collapsible buildings. The principle features of his invention were that the sections of building could be readily transported as flat packs and swiftly erected on site. Each pack had a substantial amount of electrical wiring and plumbing pre-fitted in the factory. Also each flat pack had a base and a roof, both rectangular, four pillars pivoted to the roof corners and lying horizontally between the base and roof. On erection, as the roof is lifted at the four corners, the pillars swing down by gravity so that they can be bolted to the base. Simple in concept but needing very careful design.

Our company obtained many patents home and abroad for Mr. Bolt who came to see my father every time he came up with a new development. I note that U.S. Patent No. 3284966 was filed on

16th July 1959 and after considerable argy bargy with the U.S. Patent Office examiner, was finally issued in November 1966.

As any child knows who likes keeping small creatures such as gerbils, mice and guinea pigs, the terrapin is a tortoise-like aquatic reptile which carries its house on its back. No wonder then that Mr. Bolt chose the name Terrapin as a suitable trade mark for marketing his readily transportable product. Terrapin Ltd have just celebrated 60 years of manufacturing and supplying demountable portable buildings.

Chapter 22

CONSIDERED OPINION

At each corner of a container, i.e. the type of container seen in thousands at the port of Felixstowe or on the deck of a dirty British coaster, there is a running track-shaped aperture (hole). The holes are provided for the purpose of lifting by means of a rectangular frame having twist-locks at the corners which engage the holes and are twisted through 90° into a locked position.

This was the subject matter of a patent infringement in which I was required to offer my learned opinion. The offending lifting frame was located in Swansea at the premises of Lancer Boss, famous for fork-lift trucks and tractors. I was given a demonstration in which a huge tractor with front wheels towering over me was used to manoeuvre the lifting frame over a container and to connect securely with it. (Normally, I would say 'therewith').

With the demonstration over, the directors, engineers and I assembled in the first floor board room which looked out onto the road where the demonstration had taken place. I sat with my back to the wall where I could see the giant tractor with its cab at window level, the others facing me across the board room table.

At this point of the story I am reminded of the Victorian melodrama in which the hero, who is nodding off under the influence of drink or magic mushrooms, notices each time he rouses that the cavalier's hat feathers in a painting on the wall are disappearing one by one. In my case it was each time I looked up from my papers during my deliberations, the lamp post on the opposite side of the street had gradually disappeared. Either it had moved or the tractor had! Without wishing to cause too much panic I quietly said to the managing director: "I don't wish to be alarmist but it is my opinion that that tractor seems to be moving". No lawyer makes a definitive statement.

As he turned his head to follow the line of my index finger it was as though the poor man had received a few thousand volts through his bottom. He rose from his chair as by an ejector seat, sprinted from the board room, raced down the stairs, dived through the swing doors and ran down the road to catch up with the tractor which by now was starting to gather speed. The rest of us watched from the window to admire our hero and, after he had leapt into the cab to bring the monster under control, cheered. Whatever the result of my opinion on patent infringement, I took credit for being alert.

Chapter 23

EUROPÄISCHEN PATENTAMT

In 1977 the European Patent Office in Munich, opened its doors to seven countries (now 37) which had ratified the European Patent Organisation's system enabling an applicant to file a single patent application to obtain a bunch of patents for the countries the applicant designated at the time of filing the application.

This, on the face of it, was to be a great advantage to applicants since it meant that only one application process (we call it prosecution) was necessary instead of having to convince the examiners in each of the separately selected countries' patent offices that your client's invention meets the sometimes strict legal requirements. It is not such a good idea if the EPO examiner refuses to allow the patent because in such a situation no patents would be allowed at all. Even on appeal they may still all go down the chute.

Another gauntlet to run which could result in no patents being granted at all is opposition by a third party. Once the examiner has accepted the application, this wonderful news is published in the weekly EPO Patent Bulletin and a period of nine months is allowed for a third party to lodge an opposition even if that person has no special interest, i.e. having no *locus standi*. What a nerve! A lengthy battle ensues with each side submitting heaps of documents and evidence followed by an oral hearing before the Opposition Division at the Patentamt in Munich.

It was to Munich I flew in 1990, to represent a Japanese client who had invented an improved Venetian blind having an electronic control which would store data relating to the position of the blind set by the user. Not only could the up and down setting (opening and closing) be stored as data but the angle of the blind slats too. This meant that when the blind needed to be removed for cleaning, the user could operate the blind into the fully retracted postion for ease of handling, remove the blind, and after cleaning remount the blind which, at the press of a button, would return to its stored setting with the extent of opening and angle of slats re-established. Quite useful on a large building on which many such blinds have been installed.

I rather resented my patent application having been opposed by a company which, although large and with diverse products, was not in the business of selling Venetian blinds.

It occurred to me that the panel of three examiners sitting in the court might be impressed if I could show them a sample of the blind being marketed; the subject of the invention. The clients duly obliged, contacted their Dutch distributors and the sample was delivered to my office. To my surprise it was heavy and as long as a full size pair of skis. I can vouch for the length since, in trying to fathom out how to transport the thing to Munich, I had recalled seeing an abandoned ski bag in the basement of the building where I worked. The blind fitted neatly into the ski bag. As I travelled into Munich from the airport I felt all eyes upon me. I was seen as an expert on the ski slopes and was probably about to enter the veterans' giant slalom at München Gladbach since the ski bag bore the trade mark ROSSIGNOL of skis used by the top skiers.

The patent office I attended is an impressive building and a hive of activity. The superior cafeteria demonstrated German efficiency to a tee. The lady serving me my *bratwurst und sauerkraut* spoke excellent English and left me in no doubt as to where the plates and cutlery were to be deposited after I had finished my meal. She made senior examiners in the queue cow before her.

I struggled into the court room with the ski bag and set the blind on the adjacent desk. My passport was scrutinised to make sure that I was who I said I was; only a paid up European Patent Attorney is permitted to represent the applicant, not any old Thomas, Richard or Henry, certainly not.

The court rose as the three Opposition Division panel members entered. Instructions were given regarding when to switch on the microphone and headset for the simultaneous translation delivered by interpreters peering down on the proceedings from behind sound-proof glass windows. The whole atmosphere was rather formal and had a faint hint of foreboding. I had to remind myself that this was a patent opposition hearing concerning a Venetian blind and not a criminal trial at the Old Bailey.

I wish I could claim that the success I achieved on my one and only appearance in the European Patent Office was solely due to my scintillating advocacy. After each side's arguments had been presented, the three wise men put their heads together and came up with a minor change to the wording of the patent claims whereupon the opposition was rejected and the application allowed. Upon reflection I did feel that I had an advantage over the opponents. It wasn't because of my sartorial elegance or the grey hair, it was the ski bag and an appreciation of the effort I had made to hump the heavy blind from London to Munich which had worked the magic.

Chapter 24

ADULT LITERATURE

When the shop assistant in the newsagents at Bromley South station asked my wife if she would like a brown paper bag for the magazine she had just purchased at my request, alarm bells began to ring. They had started ringing as the said magazine had been taken down from the top shelf where it had been tucked into several other magazines all coming under the heading of adult reading material. The reason for the purchase will become clear if I report the curious case of the boomerang files.

Through the London office of the New York-based publishers Penthouse, my company was asked to act as their trade mark attorneys for registering the name Penthouse and other logos in the UK and abroad. A stack of files arrived and instructions were sent to our associates to register the mark in respect of books and magazines. The reply from our New Zealand associate Mr. J. N. Hardie to our great surprise made it quite clear that he did not wish to handle 'this sort of work'. What sort of work we asked ourselves. We have never before had work turned down. By his reaction, it was as though we had sent something rather unpleasant through the post. (A US associate tells the tale of some wag putting prawns into the suitcase of a honeymoon couple who sent their luggage ahead to their hotel in Europe for their arrival several weeks later!)

Having absolutely no idea what all the fuss was about except that 'this sort of work' had signalled a hint of foreboding, my brother and I appointed my wife to purchase a copy of Penthouse magazine. We followed her into the newsagents and stood several feet behind her while the transaction was made. We stepped further away when the assistant offered her a brown paper wrapper, disassociating ourselves entirely.

The magazine was duly analysed. It was quite clearly not pornographic but the images of naked ladies with unnecessarily enhanced portions of their anatomy and discreetly placed fur pieces were quite off-putting. The advertisements for lipsticks of various shapes would not have found favour with the designs registration examiner if he adhered strictly to the letter of the law. No wonder Mr. Hardie had objected.

So the decision was made to send the stack of files back to the client's London Office with a polite letter thanking them for their custom and giving a feeble explanation for turning down the work. It did cross our minds as to what we would have done if we did not have other clients to rely on for our business. We turned down a good little earner. So that was that. Our reputation, such as it was, was re-established enabling us to carry on as upright and honest brokers. Mr. Hardie was duly thanked with accompanying apologies for the embarrassment caused and informed of the action we had taken. The matter was closed and a sigh of relief could be heard as Albert, our office maintenance man and driver, headed towards London with the spurned files.

However, there is a sequel. The files were sent by the London office back to the New York office. From there the files were taken across Manhattan to a firm of attorneys-at-law who, not being trade mark specialists, passed them on to another firm of attorneys-at-law who knew a very fine family firm of trade mark attorneys having their office in S.E. London. The boomerang files were back in our office not ten days from the moment we thought we had seen the back of them. Arghhh…!

Chapter 25

TO GRASS

I count myself fortunate in having had such excellent training as an engineer which served as a springboard to a fascinating career in patents. Daily analytical study is taxing work although well compensated by the extraordinary variety of subject matter and the moments when friendships could be forged or enhanced between like-minded people. It was like belonging to a club, something akin to Rotary International which my father so enjoyed, in which one meets friends and is welcomed almost anywhere in the world. Stone's and Matthews, Haddan brought me into contact with inventors, engineers, translators, searchers and lawyers of many countries. My visits to the United States, France, Germany, Eire, The Netherlands, Italy and Australia, have provided an abundance of happy memories of associates I have worked with.

A patent attorney friend of mine when asked what he did for a living replied that he was in the waste paper business. Now that all of the patent applications I prepared and prosecuted to grant, over the forty-eight years I practised as a patent attorney, have well and truly expired, I can understand what he meant. Furthermore, one can be critical of the whole patent system which is often argued on the one hand to be based on the human desire for gain; to obtain a monopoly for an invention and to prevent any other person from using it. On the other hand, as the argument goes, the patent system ensures that innovation is stimulated and information is made available for all the world to benefit from. Of the many thousands of patents I have obtained only a handful have been used in litigation. As in any combative situation it is better where possible to come to some agreement before fetching up in court.

Patent attorneys live in fear of missing critical dates: the law of each land is beset with dates by which documents have to be filed. A missed date usually spells disaster and the situation can rarely be retrieved if say an application lapses by mistake and publication of the invention has taken place. Form filling and meeting dates apart, the life of a patent attorney is never wanting for interest, in respect of either the subject matter as evidenced by the gamut of examples I have cited, or regarding the people we meet.

Whilst keeping my name on the Chartered Institute of Patent Attorney's list of retired members and enjoying the benefits afforded to a Fellow of the Institution of Engineering & Technology, I have, with some reluctance, dropped the qualifications of Chartered Trade Mark Attorney and European Patent Attorney. No longer are my badges nailed to the office wall; I shall rely instead upon the recently appointed Chancellor Mr. George Osborne to be generous in my golden years.

I am what is largely called 'retired' which generally implies an armchair, slippers and pipe. Contrariwise, I am never wanting for things to occupy me and am overloaded with activities which interest me. Apart from choral singing and collecting pictures, I am seen by my grandchildren as Mr. Fixit, he who can repair or construct anything wood related. I made a splendid tree-house for the grandchildren and a henhouse which was located close to the tree. Unfortunately, neither edifice was oak-tree-proof as the tree came down in a gale resulting in total demolition of both constructions along with several hens.

As to other pastimes, golf has gone (though I keep my souvenir sheered-off club head on the study wall), flying has gone (I only had one little crash—a bent nose-wheel fork, also on the study wall) and the squash racquet (not the one which broke two ribs when it came between me and the squash court wall) has not seen the light of day for a few years. However, my son Hamilton has kindly presented me with a bicycle (as well as a charming little grandson, I should add) on which I shall pedal while I can and when I can't I shall carry on scribbling until my pen or the seas gang dry. Many thanks.

POSTSCRIPT

At the Eltham College Speech Day, July 5th 2010, the presentation of prizes was made by guest of honour Major Phil Packer, former pupil of the School. On his return from Iraq, having sustained a spinal injury whilst serving in the British Army, Phil set about overcoming his disability by undertaking a number of demanding challenges including rowing the Channel and climbing Ben Nevis, Scafell Pike and Snowdon. Considerable media attention was drawn to Phil Packer in 2009 who, despite his injury, determinedly completed the London Marathon in thirteen days. In his without-notes Speech Day address he spoke enthusiastically about his charity, the British Inspiration Trust (BRIT), a multi-million pound centre of excellence to provide a residential retreat to enthuse, inspire and provide British best practice for disability. He is currently gaining support throughout the country from our leading ambassadors of sport, culture, the arts and business, to volunteer a day each year as BRIT 'mentors', to stay at the centre, and quite simply relax and inspire the disabled young people. Turning his attention to the pupils present, he exhorted them to use their abilities to the full in whatever circumstances they find themselves. Eltham College, he asserted, is very special. As I was listening to Phil speak, particularly the reference to his lack of interest in academic subjects when he was at school and accompanying apology to his teachers, my thoughts turned to my own time at Eltham and the frequent 'could do better' end-of-term teachers' reports. Whilst I like to make play in my book about my dismissal from 'the school I loved and had enjoyed', I have never harboured a grudge against the School or those who took the decision to ask me to leave. On the contrary, I have maintained an affection for Eltham since the day I left sixty-one years ago. As Major Phil says, Eltham College is very special.

PREVIOUS PUBLICATION

"You're the Doctor-You Decide
-Growing up in the Blitz

by Graham Matthews
ISBN 0-9547250-0-X